PAINT YOUR OWN
Positivity Pebbles

Published in 2024 by Two Windmills Limited

Marine House, Tide Mill Way, Woodbridge,
Suffolk, IP12 1AP, United Kingdom
www.twowindmills.com

Text, design and layout copyright © 2024 Two Windmills Limited
Illustration copyright © 2024 Two Windmills Limited/Shutterstock.com

All rights reserved. No part of this publication may be reproduced, stored in a retrieval system, or transmitted in any form or by any means, electronically, mechanical, photocopying, recording or otherwise, without the prior permission of the copyright owners and the publishers.

A CIP catalogue record for this book is available from the British Library.

EU Authorised Representative, Vulcan Consulting,
38/39 Fitzwilliam Square West, Dublin 2, D02 NX53, Ireland

Printed in Guangdong, China

10 9 8 7 6 5 4 3 2 1

Positivity Rocks!

Cute, cool and oozing with feel-good energy, painting positive pebbles is the most mindful craft craze around. Get ready to share the lighter side of life and learn how to transform pebbles into colourful, life-affirming works of art from the heart!

In your kit

In your kit you'll find everything you need to get started straight away. There are six pebbles that have been rubbed smooth by rivers over hundreds of years, acrylic paints, paintbrushes, and stickers for added decoration.

Pebbles

In different shapes and sizes.

Paintbrushes

Remember to clean them when you change colours!

Acrylic paints

With bold, bright and positive colours!

Stickers

To jazz up your designs.

Inspiration!

At the back of the book you'll find an inspiration gallery of pebble design ideas, spaces to collect positive quotes and pages for sketching and doodling your own great ideas!

Before You Start

Pebbles may be hard, but pebble painting doesn't have to be. The illustrated pebbles in this book are really just a guide. If you feel confident, you can paint your pebbles in whatever colours and designs you like. As well as the items in your kit, you'll need to gather together a few more things before you start.

Newspaper
Use this to cover your work surface.

Paper plate
Use for mixing your colours.

Glass of water
Use this for cleaning your brushes in between each colour.

Kitchen towel
Use this for drying your brushes and keeping your work area clean and tidy.

If you get the pebble painting bug you'll want to buy some more acrylic paint and find some more pebbles. Beaches are a good place to find pebbles, but keep your eyes peeled and you'll find them everywhere! You can buy acrylic paint in craft or hobby shops, or online.

 Be careful

- Keep paints and pebbles away from small children and pets.

- Always take an adult with you when you go looking for pebbles.

- It's a good idea to rinse and dry your pebbles before you start.

- When you have finished painting, put everything away safely for next time.

Sharing is Caring

Painting onto pebbles isn't new! Humans have been doing it for hundreds of thousands of years. However, the trend to paint a positive pebble and to then hide it for someone else to find is much more recent!

When you've finished the designs in this book, hide your pebble on a trail, at the beach, or in a park so it gives someone a little lift when they find it. Who knows what they'll achieve with the positive energy they get from your art!

Positivity Tip
Always hide your pebbles in a place where it is safe for someone to stop and look at them!

Love Heart (easy)

A bright base colour with a contrasting motif and heartfelt message are the core elements of this creative design. Spread some love!

- Paint your pebble or pebbles all over with a bright base colour.

- When the base colour is dry, use a contrasting colour to paint a heart shape in the centre of the pebble.

- Use white paint to add dots around the heart shape.

- Use a contrasting colour of paint to add a positive message to your Heart Art design.

Positivity Tip

Consider which colours to use before you start. Sometimes, just two or three can be really striking.

Positive Pebbles Messages for this project:

- Spread Love
- Love Yourself!
- Love Rules!
- Love Life!

Good Vibrations (easy)

Finding inspiration for your art doesn't have to be hard! Sometimes all you need is a strong word or message and bold colours. Imagine finding one of these pebbles. It would be sure to brighten up your day!

- Paint your pebble or pebbles all over with a bright base colour. You can mix things up by painting a multicoloured base colour - the only limit to the colours you can use is your imagination!

- When the base colour is dry, use a contrasting colour to paint a simple uplifting message.

- Use a contrasting colour of paint to add delicate dots, spots or stripes to your designs. Simple!

Positivity Tip

Less can be more! If modern minimalism is your thing, strong messages work just as well on white pebbles.

Positive Pebbles Messages for this project:

- Family
- Breathe
- You got this!
- Laugh
- Smile
- Brave
- Be happy
- Pray
- Shine
- Be kind
- Peace
- Trust

Rainbows Rock! (medium)

Now more than ever, rainbows have come to be a sign of support, of resilience and of hope. The greater the storm, the brighter the rainbow.

Show that you care by leaving this stunning rainbow-themed pebble for someone to find.

- Rainbows are made up of seven colours, but we've used six for this design.

- Apply the six colours in bands across your rock. Allow each colour to dry before applying the next band.

- Use blue to paint a heart shape that extends over the entire pebble.

- Use white paint to add polka dot detail to the heart-shaped band.

Positivity Tip

Balance this pebble on a plant so its caring colours shine! A sturdy succulent will hold the weight of your pebble perfectly.

Mindful Mandalas (advanced)

Mandalas have been around for many hundreds of years and are used by many different religions and cultures to aid prayer and promote mindfulness.

These designs are for inspiration only. Start with a central circle or dot and work your way outwards to represent our ever-expanding universe!

- Paint your pebble in a base colour of your choice. Darker colours can often work best and will make subsequent colours pop! Allow to dry.

- Use a colour that contrasts with the background to paint a circle in the middle of your pebble.

- Clean your brush and use a different colour to paint additional circles around the central one. Leave space around them.

- Now start adding smaller dots around each circle. Using the same colour can help to tie the design together.

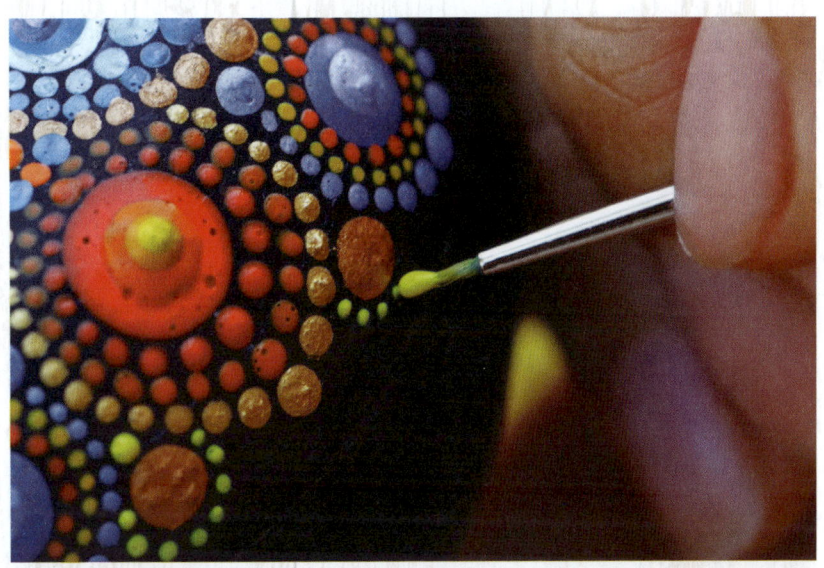

- Gradually work your way out to the edge of your pebble, changing colours of paint to create additional circles as you go.

- Make sure you surround each large circle with dots of the same colour to make it really stand out. This detailed work can be calming and mindful in itself. Relax!

Positivity Tip

Don't put too much paint onto the brush. Build up colour intensity in layers until you achieve the look you want!

Storage Ideas

When the weather is bad or life is too busy, sometimes you'll need somewhere safe to store your pebble designs. What could be better than an upcycled glass food jar topped with a delicate pebble design?

- Keep and clean out glass jars that contained food items such as jam, syrup, vegetables and more - as long as it has a lid and a wide neck it's a keeper!

- Remove any labels from the jar by soaking in hot water.

- When dry, use acrylic paint to paint a base layer of colour over the entire lid. If the lid is already coloured and does not contain manufacturer writing you could leave it as it is.

- Use a contrasting colour of acrylic paint to paint a mandala or other shape-based design onto your jar. Less is more!

- Find a small pebble and paint a design that closely matches the one on the lid. The design should be simple so as not to detract from the works of art that you'll store in the jar.

- Use strong glue to attach the small painted pebble onto the lid of the jar.

- Use the jar to store your positivity pebble designs before sharing them with the world.

Sometimes you'll love your pebble designs so much that you want to keep them. This glass storage project is a great way to show off your favourite designs.

Limitless!

The only limit to your positive pebble creativity is your imagination! The following pages contain a gallery of great designs that you can follow or use for inspiration. Get creative and share the positivity!

Animals

"Believe you can and you are halfway there."
Theodore Roosevelt

Animals

"Nothing is impossible. The word itself says 'I'm possible.'"
Audrey Hepburn

Slogans

"Try to be a rainbow in someone else's cloud."
Maya Angelou

Patterns

"It isn't where you came from.
It's where you're going
that counts."
Ella Fitzgerald

Halloween

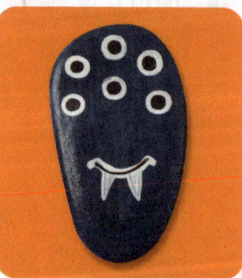

"*It always seems impossible until it is done.*"
Nelson Mandela

Christmas

"Happiness is not by chance, but by choice."
Jim Rohn

Home

"Some people look for a beautiful place. Others make a place beautiful."
Hazrat Khan

Unicorns

"Do what you can with what you have, wherever you are."
Theodore Roosevelt

Dinosaurs

"Follow your own passion. Not your parents. Not your teachers'. Yours!"
Robert Ballard

Mandalas

"Keep your face to the sunshine and you cannot see a shadow."
— Helen Keller

Seaside

"You don't have to be great to start, but you have to start to be great."
Zig Ziglar

Birds

"Look at the world through rainbow-coloured glasses."
Anon

Things I Love

"Positive anything is better than negative nothing."
Elbert Hubbard

"The greater the storm, the brighter the rainbow."
Anon

Favourite Quotes and Memes

Use the following pages to make a note of your favourite empowering quotes and memes that will brighten up someone's day if they saw them painted on a pebble. The quotes could be from famous authors, movie stars, or just something that you overheard whilst shopping!

Favourite Quotes and Memes

Favourite Quotes and Memes

My Positivity Pebble Design Ideas

Every artist starts with a blank canvas! Use these pages to sketch, doodle and design your own ideas for positive pebble works of art.

My Positivity Pebble Design Ideas

My Positivity Pebble Design Ideas